62 FAVORITE HYMNS
for big note piano
Arranged by Richard Bradley

MW00895648

✝✝✝✝✝✝✝✝✝✝✝✝✝✝✝✝✝✝✝✝✝✝✝✝✝✝✝✝✝✝✝✝✝✝✝✝

Bradley
Publications
a division of
RBR Communications, Inc.

Amazing Grace

Words by
JOHN NEWTON and
JOHN P. REES

AMERICAN MELODY
Arranged by Richard Bradley

What A Friend We Have In Jesus

Words and Music by
JOSEPH SCRIVEN and
CHARLES C. CONVERSE
Arranged by Richard Bradley

What A Friend We Have In Jesus - 2 - 1

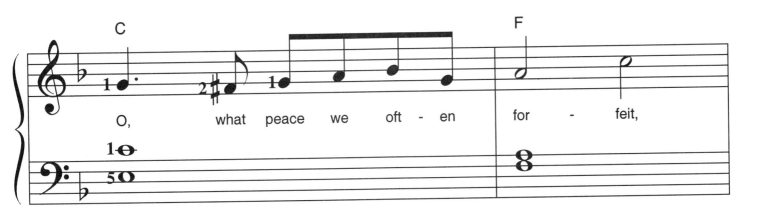

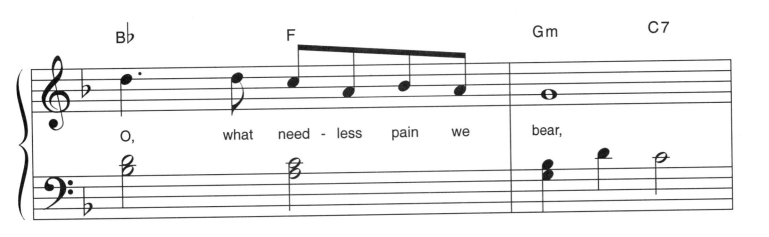

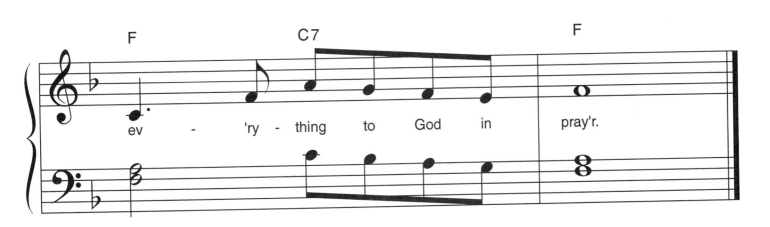

Jesus Loves Me!

Words and Music by
ANNA WARNER and
WILLIAM BRADBURY
Arranged by Richard Bradley

God Is So Good

TRADITIONAL
Arranged by Richard Bradley

God Is So Good - 1 - 1

I Love To Tell The Story

Words and Music by
KATHERINE HANKEY
and WILLIAM G. FISCHER
Arranged by Richard Bradley

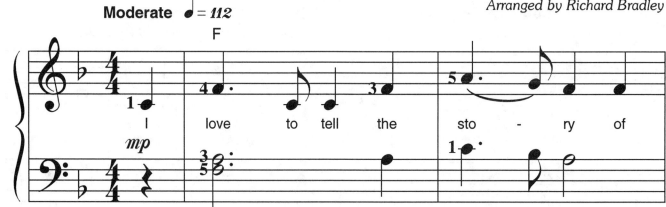

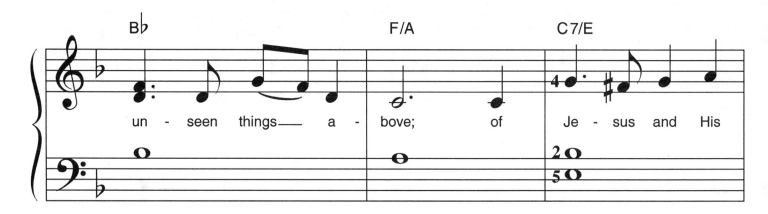

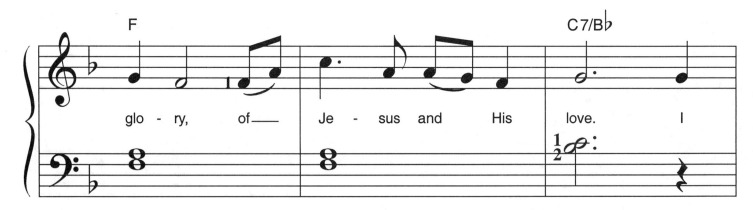

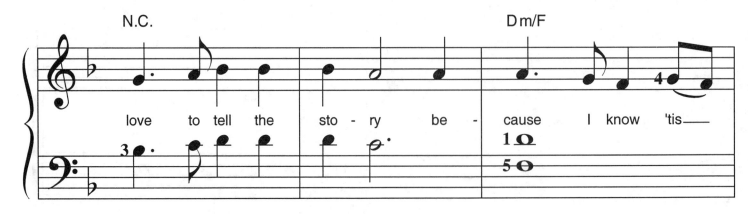

I Love To Tell The Story - 2 - 1

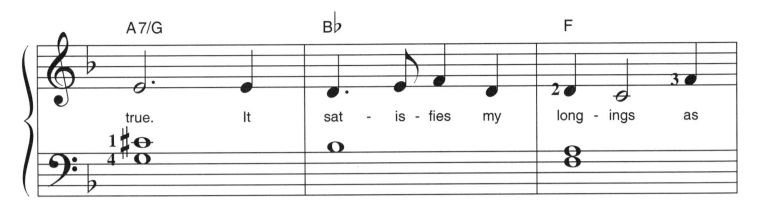

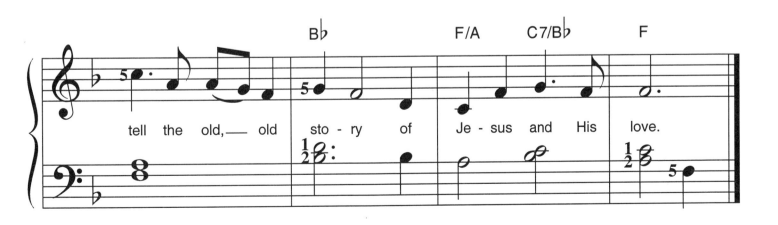

We Gather Together To Ask The Lord's Blessing

TRADITIONAL
Arranged by Richard Bradley

We Gather Together To Ask The Lord's Blessing - 1 - 1

Deep And Wide

TRADITIONAL
Arranged by Richard Bradley

Deep And Wide - 1 - 1

The Church In The Wildwood

By
W. S. PITTS
Arranged by Richard Bradley

The Church In The Wildwood - 2 - 2

Rock Of Ages

AUGUSTUS MONTAGUE TOPLADY
and THOMAS HASTINGS
Arranged by Richard Bradley

Heavenly Sunshine

Words and Music by
H.J. ZELLEY and
GEORGE H. COOKE
Arranged by Richard Bradley

Blessed Assurance

Words and Music by
FANNY CROSBY VAN ALSTYNE
and MRS. JOSEPH F. KNAPP
Arranged by Richard Bradley

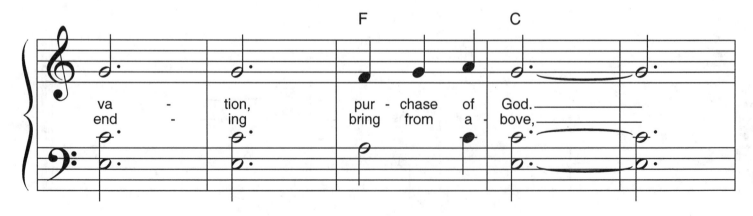

Blessed Assurance - 3 - 1

18

Fairest Lord Jesus
(Crusaders' Hymn)

TRADITIONAL
Arranged by Richard Bradley

Love Divine

CHARLES WESLEY
and JOHN ZUNDEL
Arranged by Richard Bradley

Love Divine - 2 - 1

The B-I-B-L-E

TRADITIONAL
Arranged by Richard Bradley

The B-I-B-L-E - 1 - 1

Nearer, My God, To Thee

Words and Music by
SARAH FLOWER ADAMS
and LOWELL MASON
Arranged by Richard Bradley

Moderate ♩ = 112

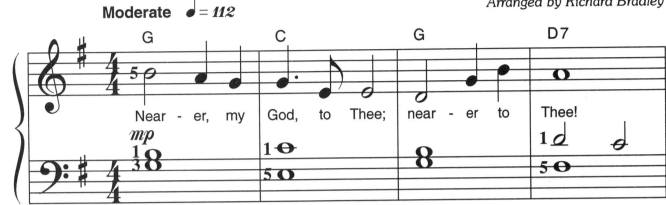

Near - er, my God, to Thee; near - er to Thee!

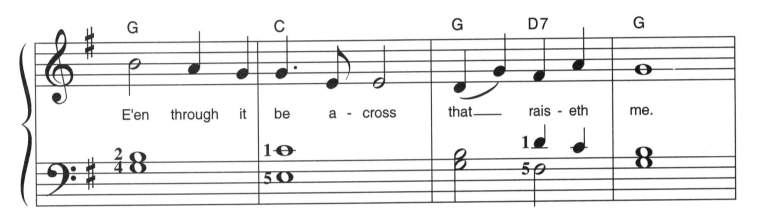

E'en through it be a - cross that raiseth me.

Still all my song shall be, near - er, my God, to Thee.

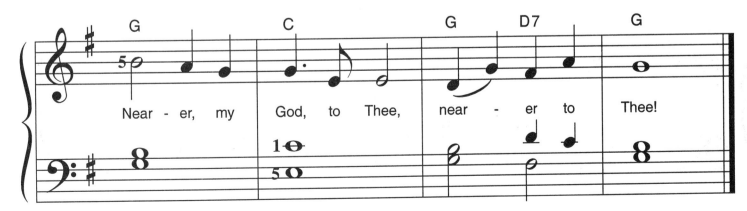

Near - er, my God, to Thee, near - er to Thee!

Nearer, My God, To Thee - 1 - 1

Wonderful Words Of Life

By
PHILLIP P. BLISS
Arranged by Richard Bradley

Abide With Me

Words and Music by
HENRY FRANCIS LYLE
and WILLIAM HENRY MONK
Arranged by Richard Bradley

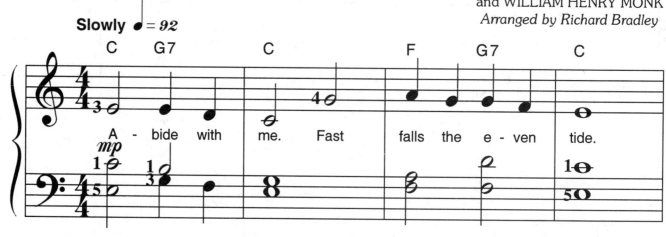

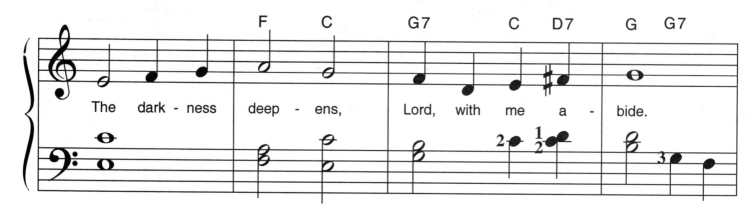

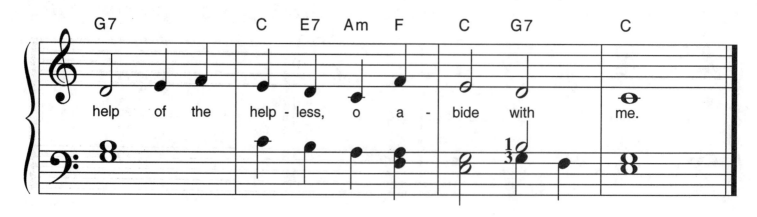

Abide With Me - 1 - 1

For The Beauty Of The Earth

FOLLIOTT S. PIERPONT
and CONRAD KOCHER
Arranged by Richard Bradley

In The Sweet Bye-And-Bye

Words and Music by
S. FILLMORE BENNETT
and J. P. WEBSTER
Arranged by Richard Bradley

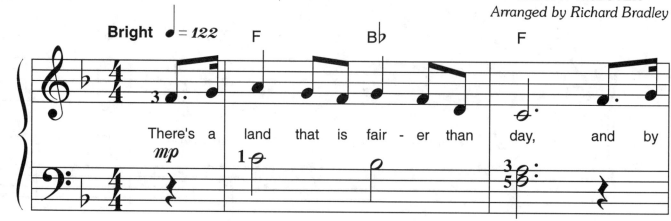

There's a land that is fair - er than day, and by

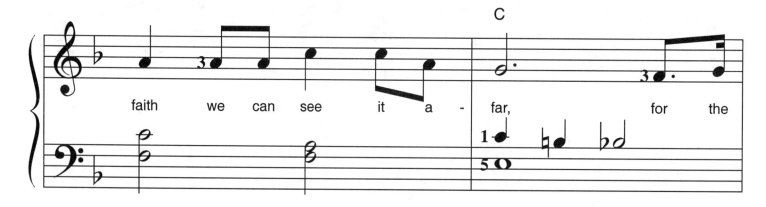

faith we can see it a - far, for the

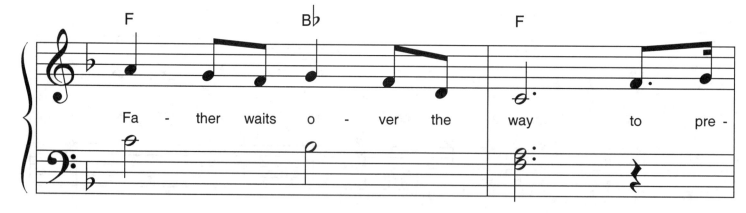

Fa - ther waits o - ver the way to pre -

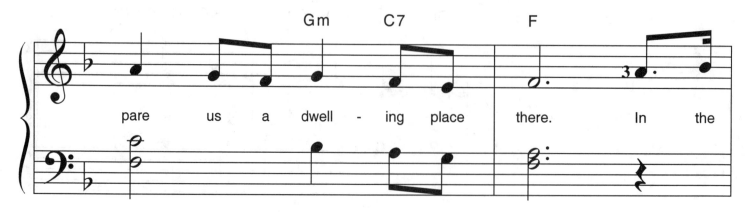

pare us a dwell - ing place there. In the

Rise And Shine

SPIRITUAL
Arranged by Richard Bradley

This Little Light Of Mine

TRADITIONAL
Arranged by Richard Bradley

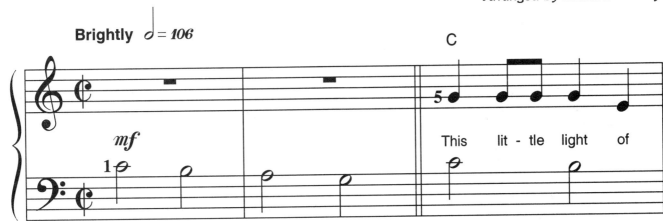

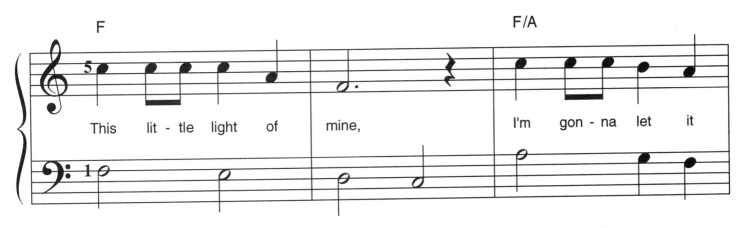

This Little Light Of Mine - 1 - 1

Bringing In The Sheaves

Words and Music by
KNOWLES SHAW
and GEORGE A. MINOR
Arranged by Richard Bradley

33

Jesus Loves The Little Children

Words and Music by
GEORGE F. ROOT
Arranged by Richard Bradley

Jesus Loves The Little Children - 1 - 1

Oh, How I Love Jesus

Words by
FREDERICK WHITFIELD

AMERICAN MELODY
Arranged by Richard Bradley

He Leadeth Me

JOSEPH H. GILMORE
and WILLIAM B. BRADBURY
Arranged by Richard Bradley

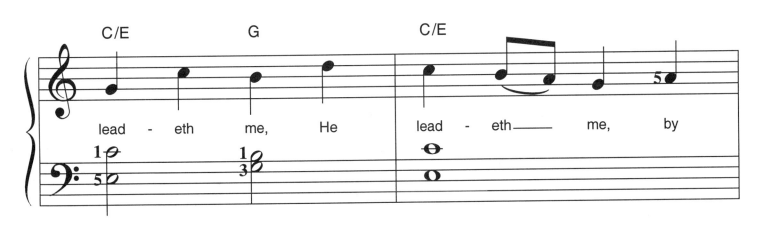

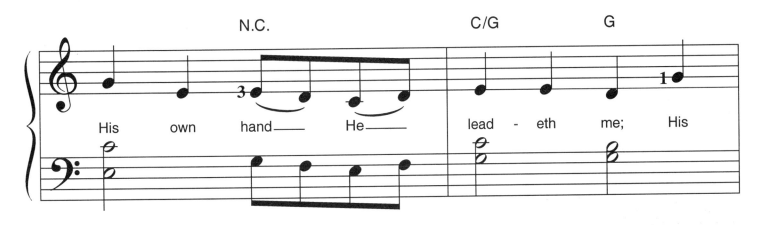

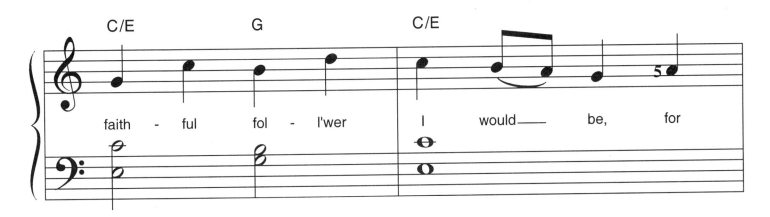

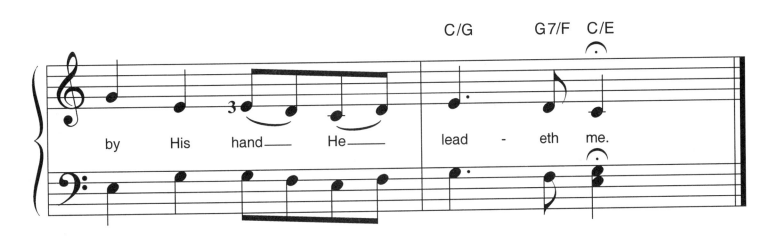

Kum Ba Yah
(Come By Here)

TRADITIONAL SPIRITUAL
Arranged by Richard Bradley

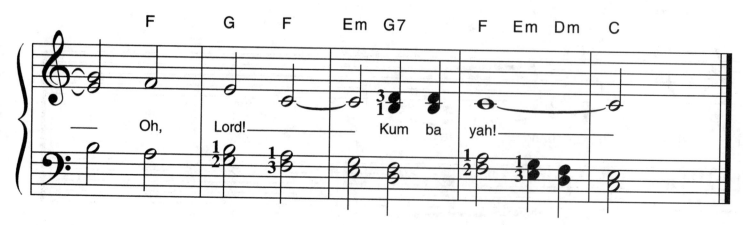

Kum Ba Yah - 1 - 1

Go Down Moses

TRADITIONAL
Arranged by Richard Bradley

All Things Bright And Beautiful

By
CECIL F. ALEXANDER
Arranged by Richard Bradley

Moderate ♩ = 118

Lyrics: All things bright and beau-ti-ful, all crea-tures great and small. All things wise and won-der-ful, the Lord God made them all. Each lit-tle flower that o-pens, each lit-tle bird that sings, He

All Things Bright And Beautiful - 2 - 1

Climb, Climb Up Sunshine Mountain

TRADITIONAL
Arranged by Richard Bradley

O Master, Let Me Walk With Thee

WASHINGTON GLADDEN
and H. PERCY SMITH
Arranged by Richard Bradley

O Master, Let Me Walk With Thee - 1 - 1

Were You There?

TRADITIONAL
Arranged by Richard Bradley

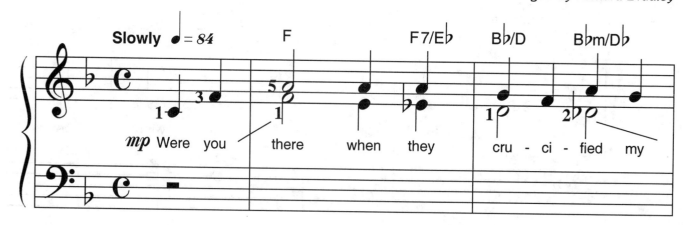

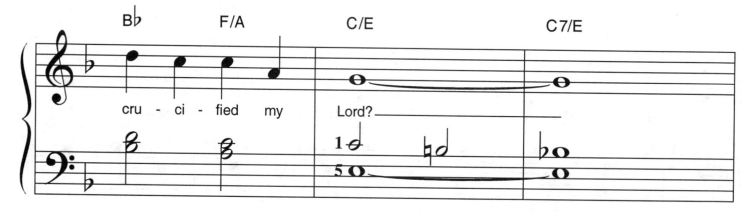

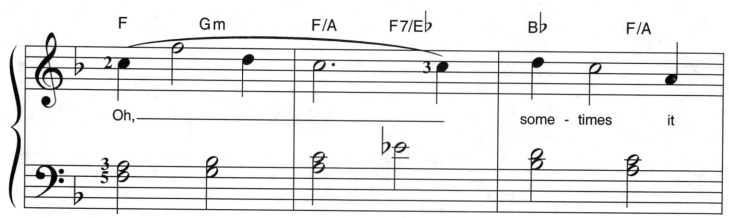

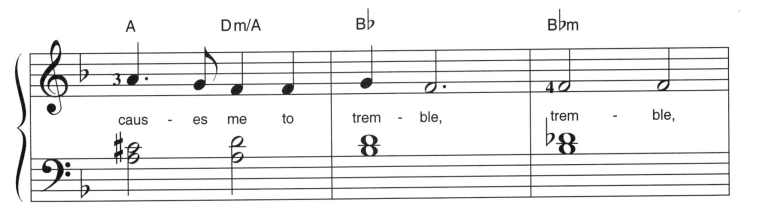

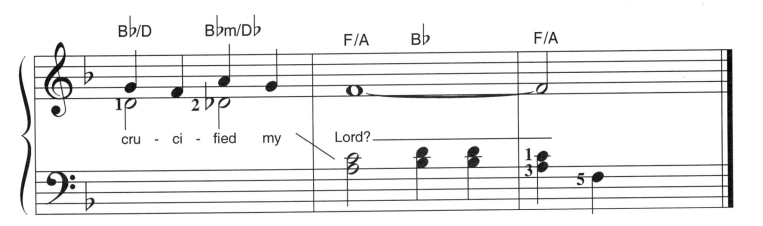

Verse 2:
Were you there when they nailed Him to the tree?
Were you there when they nailed Him to the tree?
Oh, sometimes it causes me to tremble, tremble, tremble.
Were you there when they nailed Him to the tree?

Verse 3:
Were you there when they laid Him in the tomb?
Were you there when they laid Him in the tomb?
Oh, sometimes it causes me to tremble, tremble, tremble.
Were you there when they laid Him in the tomb?

Verse 4:
Were you there when He rose up from the dead?
Were you there when He rose up from the dead?
Oh, sometimes it causes me to tremble, tremble, tremble.
Were you there when He rose up from the dead?

I Have The Joy

Words and Music by
GEORGE W. COOKE
Arranged by Richard Bradley

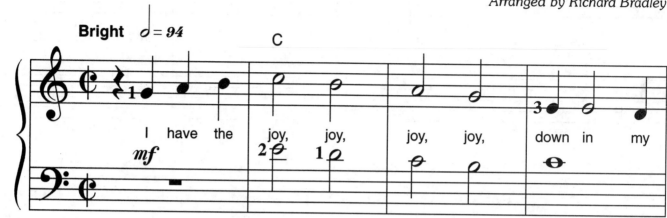

I Have The Joy - 1 - 1

Jesus Loves Even Me

PHILLIP P. BLISS
Arranged by Richard Bradley

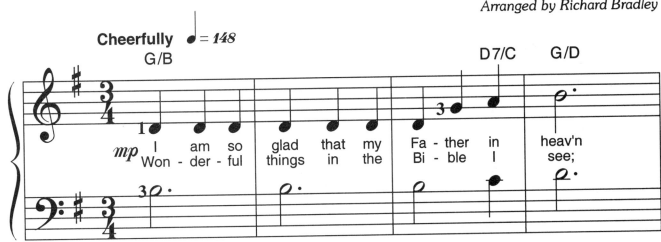

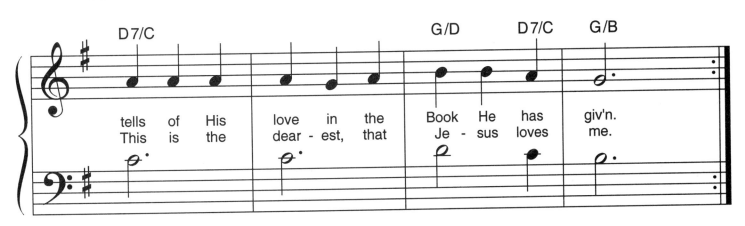

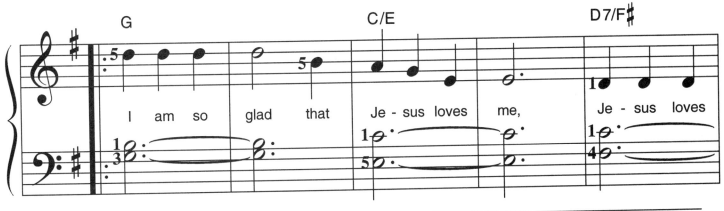

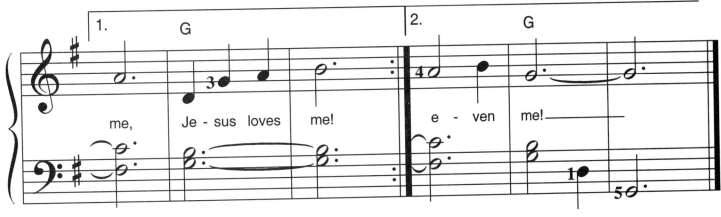

Jesus Loves Even Me - 1 - 1

Onward, Christian Soldiers

Lyric by
SABINE BARING-GOULD

Music by
SIR ARTHUR S. SULLIVAN
Arranged by Richard Bradley

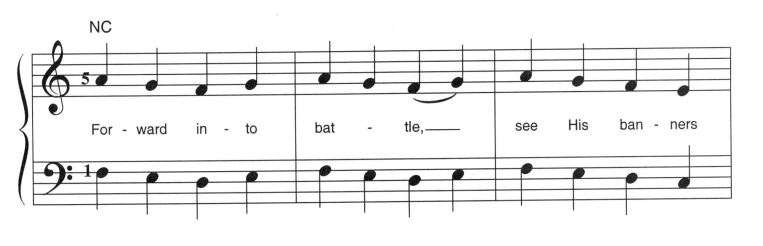

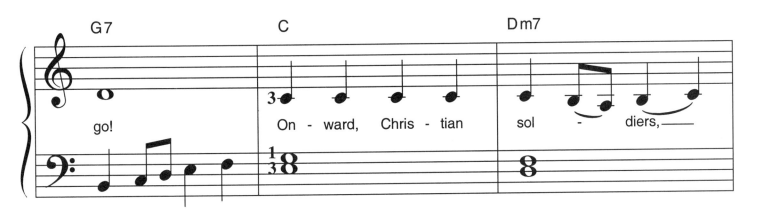

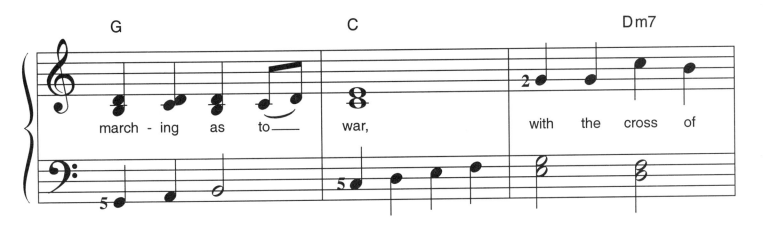

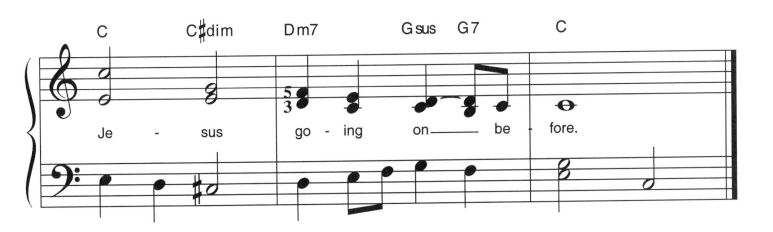

Christ Arose

ROBERT LOWRY
Arranged by Richard Bradley

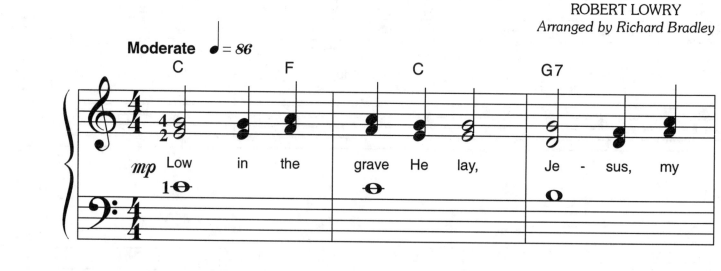

Moderate ♩ = 86

Low in the grave He lay, Je - sus, my

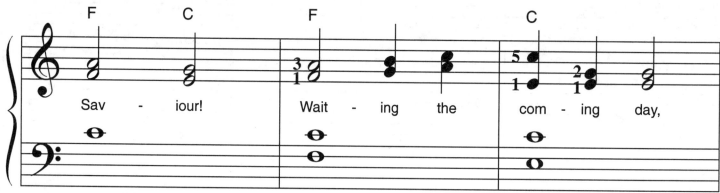

Sav - iour! Wait - ing the com - ing day,

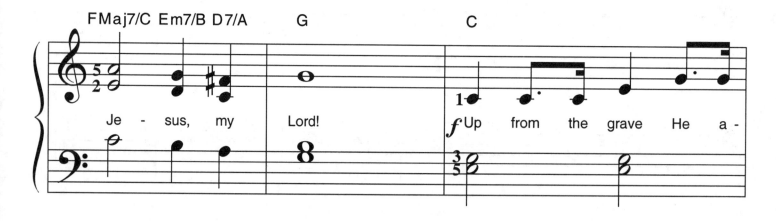

Je - sus, my Lord! Up from the grave He a -

rose, (He a - rose!) with a might - y tri - umph o'er His

We Are Climbing Jacob's Ladder

TRADITIONAL
Arranged by Richard Bradley

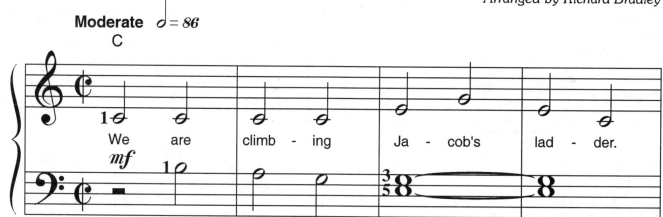

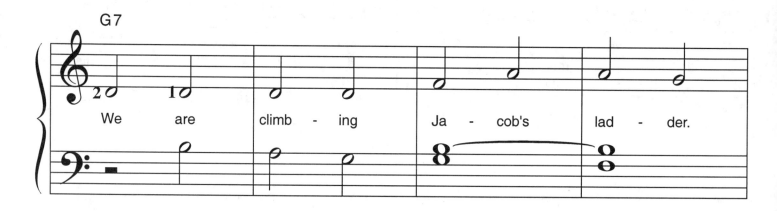

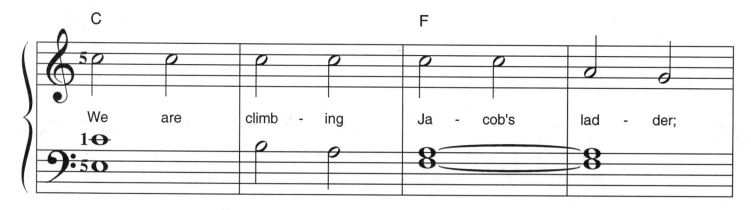

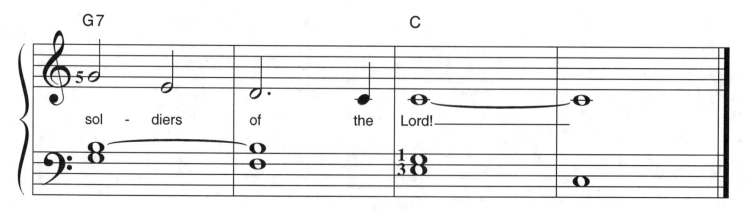

We Are Climbing Jacob's Ladder - 1 - 1

Hear Our Prayer, O Lord

TRADITIONAL
Arranged by Richard Bradley

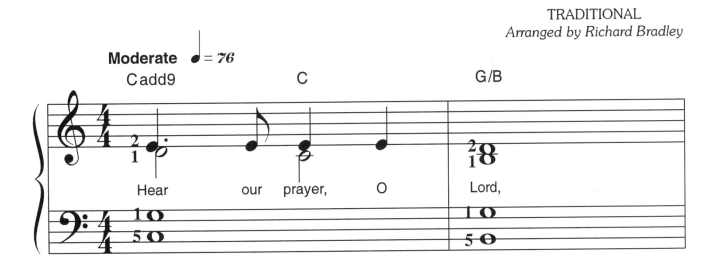

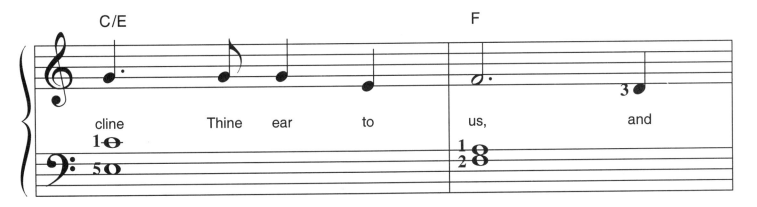

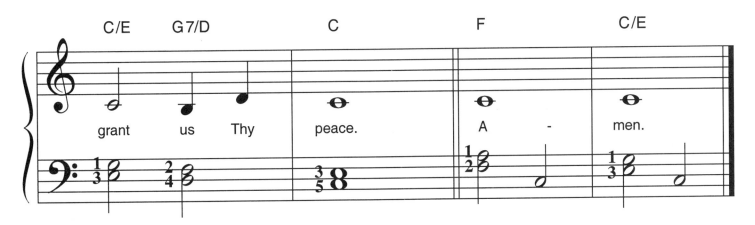

Hear Our Prayer - 1 - 1

I'll Be A Sunbeam

Words and Music by
NELLIE TALBOT and
EDWIN O. EXCELL
Arranged by Richard Bradley

Moderate ♩ = 122

Je - sus wants me for a sun - beam, to shine on Him each day; In ev - 'ry way try to please Him, at home, at school, at play.

I'll Be A Sunbeam - 2 - 1

A Mighty Fortress Is Our God

MARTIN LUTHER
Arranged by Richard Bradley

Come Into His Presence Singing

TRADITIONAL
Arranged by Richard Bradley

Verse 2:
Come into His presence singing
Jesus is Lord, Jesus is Lord, Jesus is Lord.
Verse 3:
Praise the Lord together singing
Worthy the Lamb, worthy the Lamb, worthy the Lamb.
Verse 4:
Praise the Lord together singing
Glory to God, glory to God, glory to God.

Come Into His Presence Singing - 1 - 1

Doxology
(Old Hundredth)

LOUIS BOURGEOIS
Arranged by Richard Bradley

Doxology - 1 - 1

Hallelujah!

TRADITIONAL
Arranged by Richard Bradley

Hallelujah! - 2 - 1

Jesus Is Calling

Words by
FANNY J. CROSBY

Music by
GEORGE C. STEBBINS
Arranged by Richard Bradley

Jesus Is Calling - 2 - 1

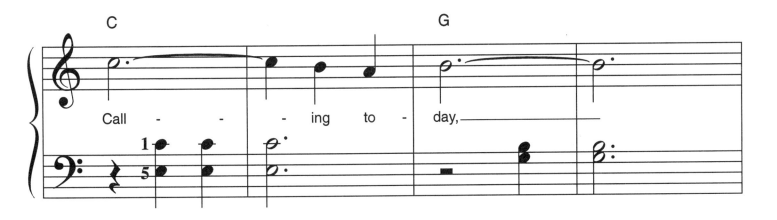

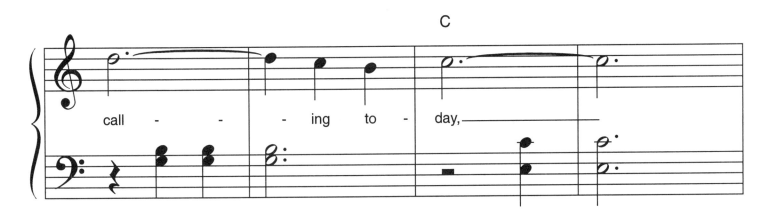

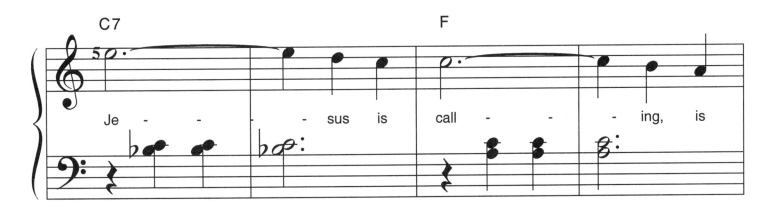

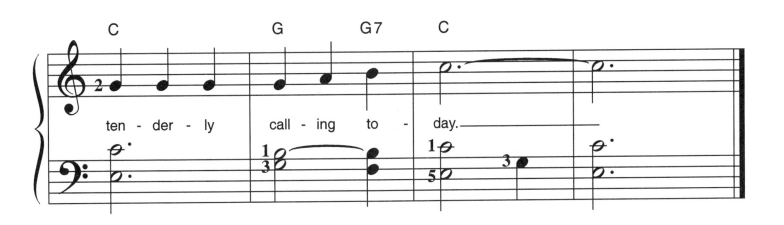

Holy, Holy, Holy

Words and Music by
REGINALD HEBER
and JOHN B. DYKES
Arranged by Richard Bradley

Blest Be The Tie That Binds

JOHN FAWCETT
and HANS GEORG NAGELI
Arranged by Richard Bradley

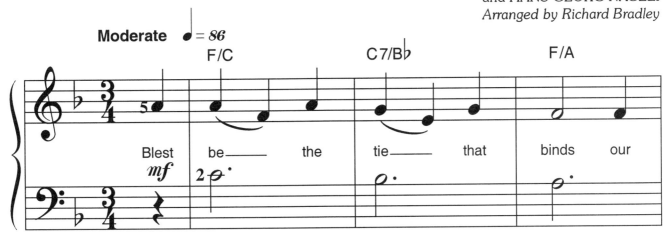

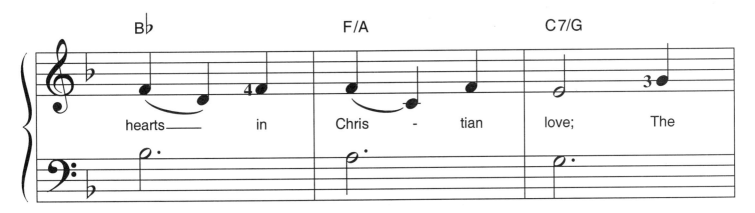

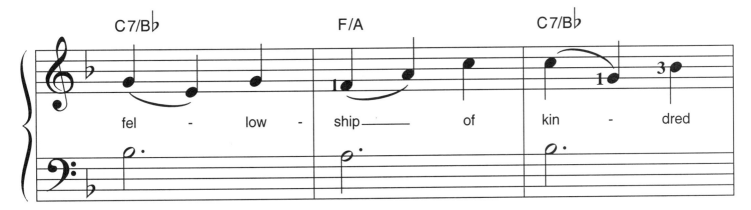

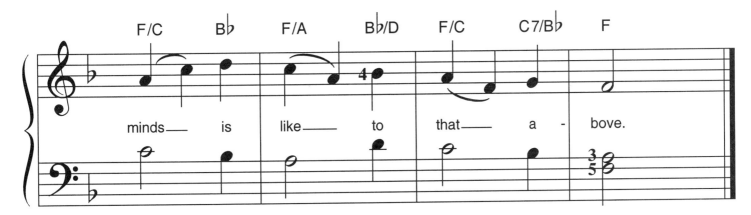

Blest Be The Tie That Binds - 1 - 1

Faith Of Our Fathers

Words and Music by
FREDERICK W. FABER
and HENRI F. HEMY
Arranged by Richard Bradley

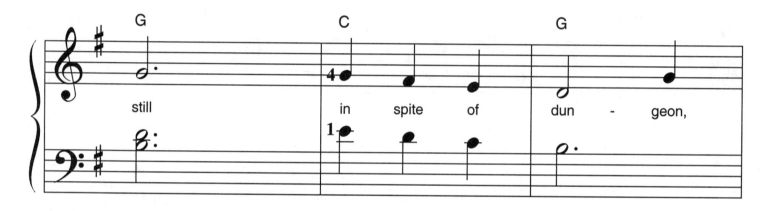

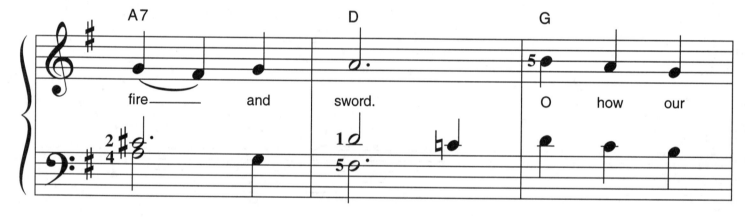

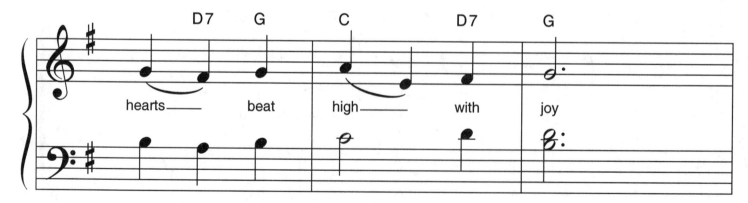

Faith Of Our Fathers - 2 - 1

67

Faith Of Our Fathers - 2 - 2

Sweet Hour Of Prayer

Words and Music by
WILLIAM W, WALFORD and
WILLIAM B. BRADBURY
Arranged by Richard Bradley

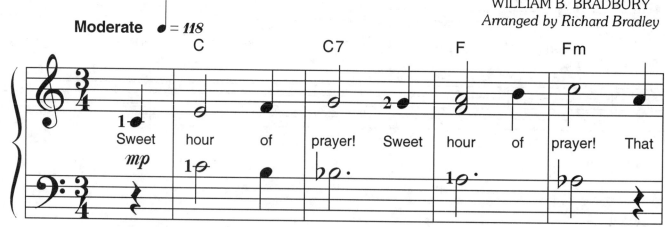

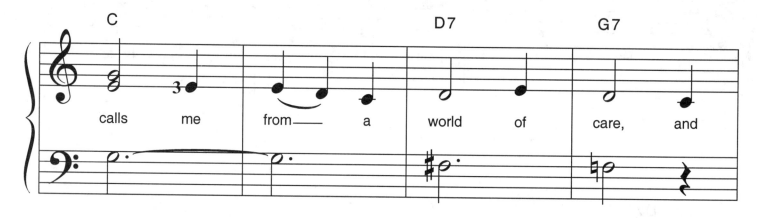

Sweet Hour Of Prayer - 2 - 1

Oh, Be Careful

TRADITIONAL
Arranged by Richard Bradley

Oh, Be Careful - 2 - 1

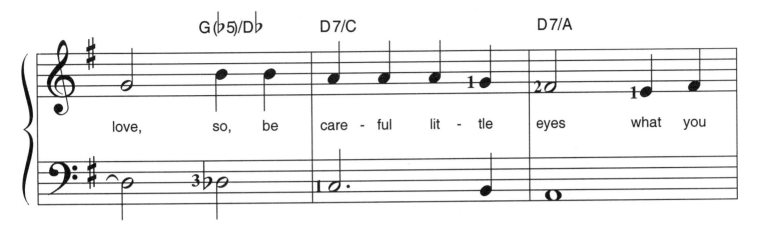

2. Oh, be careful little ears what you hear.

3. Oh, be careful little hands what you do.

4. Oh, be careful little feet where you go.

5. Oh, be careful little heart whom you trust.

6. Oh, be careful little mind what you think.

The Lord Is My Shepherd

MONTGOMERY
and KOSCHAT
Arranged by Richard Bradley

The Lord Is My Shepherd - 2 - 1

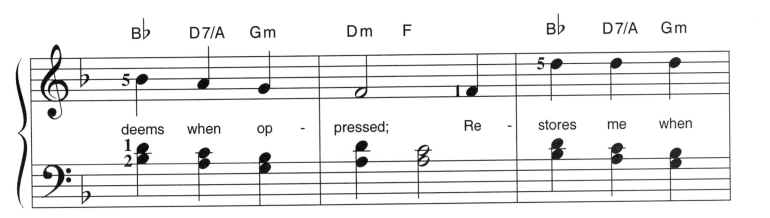

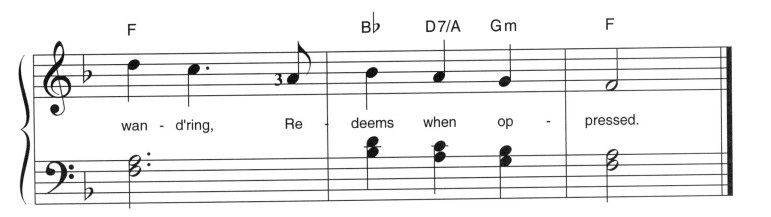

The Lord Is My Shepherd - 2 - 2

Come And Go With Me

TRADITIONAL
Arranged by Richard Bradley

Come, Thou Almighty King

FELICE de GIARDINI
Arranged by Richard Bradley

Come, Thou Al- might - ty King, Help us Thy name_____ to sing; Help us to praise: Fa - ther, all glo - ri - ous, O'er all vic - to - ri - ous, Come and reign o - ver us, An - cient of Days.

Come, Thou Almighty King - 1 - 1

America
(My Country 'Tis Of Thee)

SAMUEL F. SMITH
and HENRY CAREY
Arranged by Richard Bradley

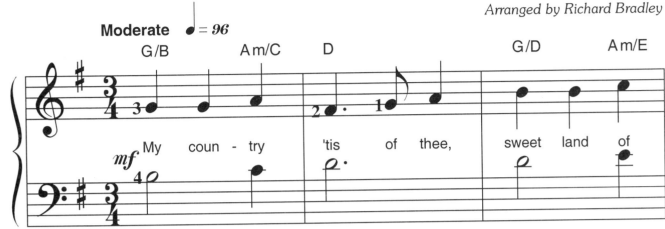

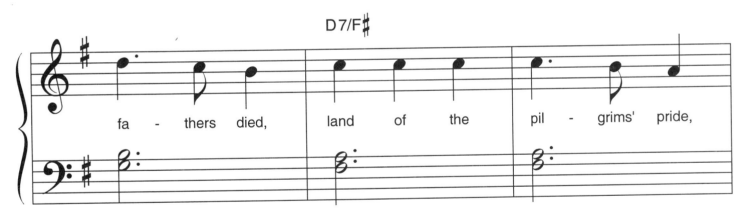

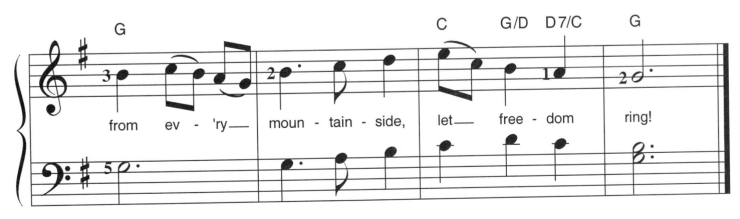

America - 1 - 1

The Battle Hymn Of The Republic

Words and Music by
WILLIAM STEFFE and
JULIA WARD HOWE
Arranged by Richard Bradley

March style ♩ = 82

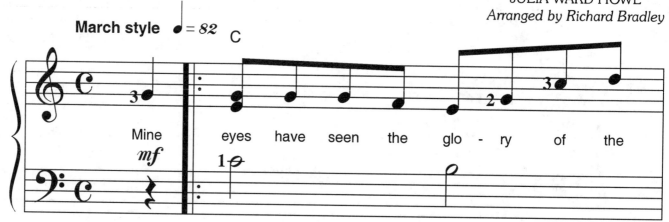

Mine eyes have seen the glo - ry of the

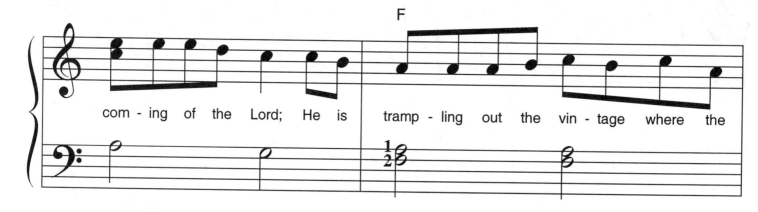

com - ing of the Lord; He is tramp - ling out the vin - tage where the

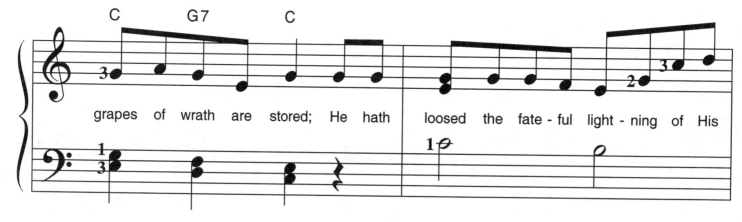

grapes of wrath are stored; He hath loosed the fate - ful light - ning of His

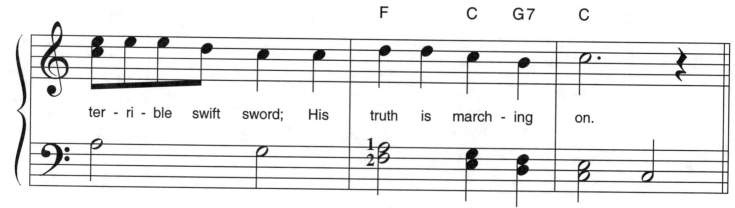

ter - ri - ble swift sword; His truth is march - ing on.

The Battle Hymn Of The Republic - 2 - 1

Additional Lyric:
I have seen Him in the watchfires
Of a hundred circling camps;
They have builded Him an altar
In the evening dews and damps;
I can read His righteous sentence
By their dim and flaring lamps;
His truth is marching on.

My God Is So Great

TRADITIONAL
Arranged by Richard Bradley

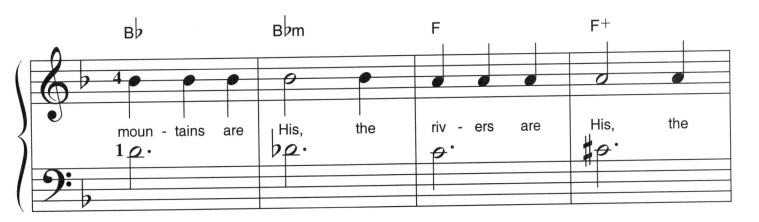

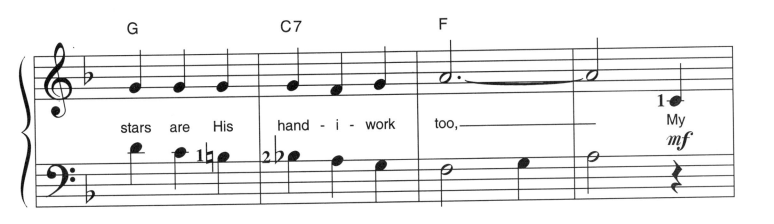

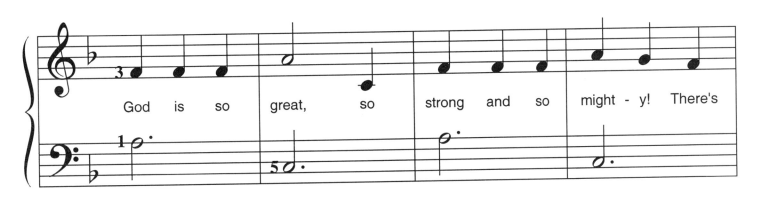

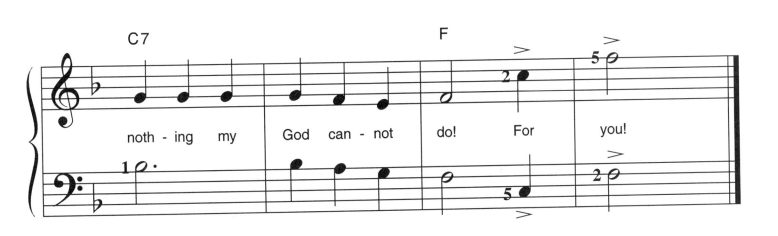

Joshua Fought The Battle Of Jericho

TRADITIONAL
Arranged by Richard Bradley

Joshua Fought The Battle Of Jericho - 2 - 1

I've Got Peace Like A River

AFRO-AMERICAN SPIRITUAL
Arranged by Richard Bradley

I've Got Peace Like A River - 2 - 1

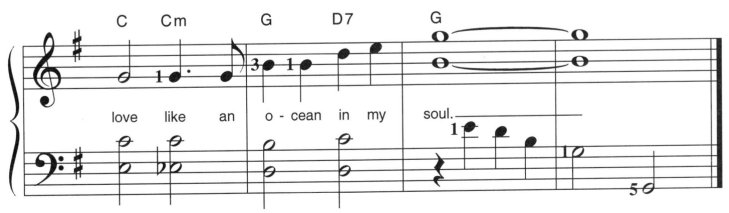

I've Got Peace Like A River - 2 - 2

God Be With You

Words and Music by
JEREMIAH E. RANKIN and
WILLIAM G. TOMER
Arranged by Richard Bradley

God Be With You - 2 - 1

God Be With You - 2 - 2

Do Lord

TRADITIONAL SPIRITUAL
Arranged by Richard Bradley

Moderate ♩ = 148

I've got a home in glo-ry land that out-shines the sun,

I've got a home in glo-ry land that out-shines the sun,

I've got a home in glo-ry land that out-shines the sun, look a-

way be-yond the blue.

Do Lord - 2 - 1

Come, Thou Fount

ROBERT ROBINSON
and JOHN WYETH
Arranged by Richard Bradley

Come, Thou Fount - 2 - 1

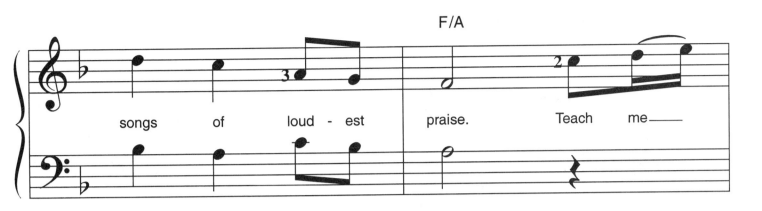

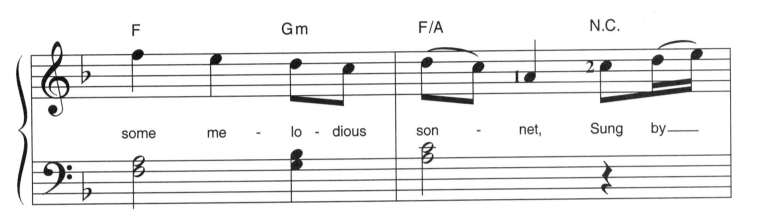

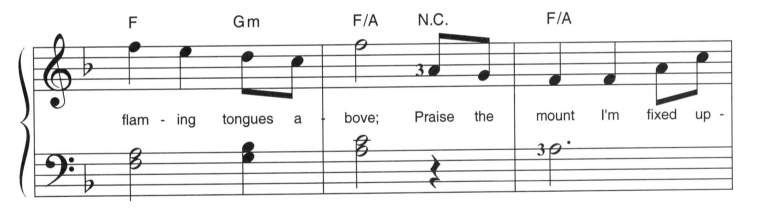

The Church's One Foundation

SAMUEL J. STONE and
SAMUEL SEBASTIAN WESLEY
Arranged by Richard Bradley

The Church's One Foundation - 2 - 1

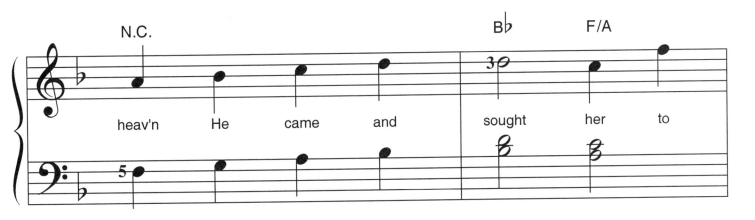

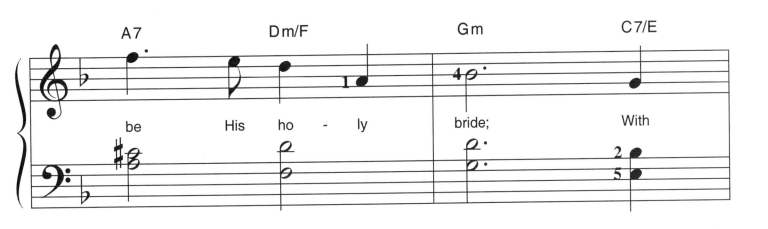

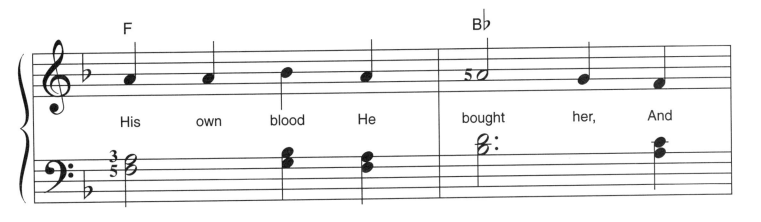

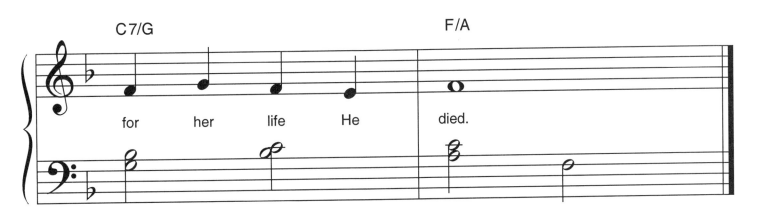

Christ, The Lord, Is Risen Today

CHARLES WESLEY
Arranged by Richard Bradley

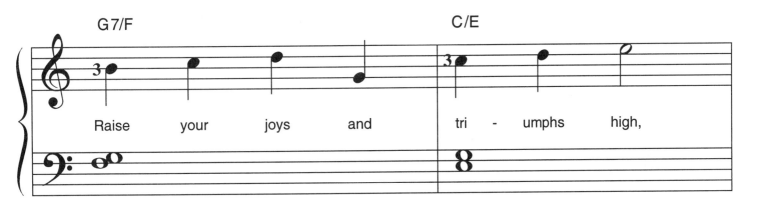
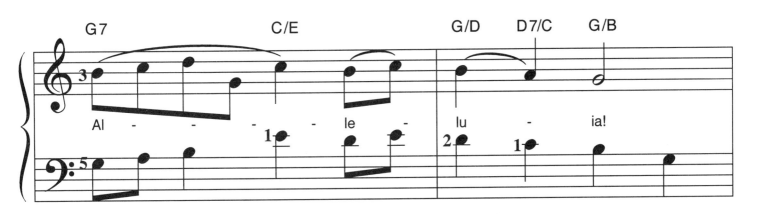
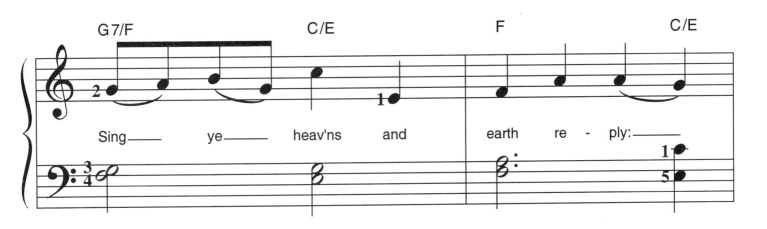
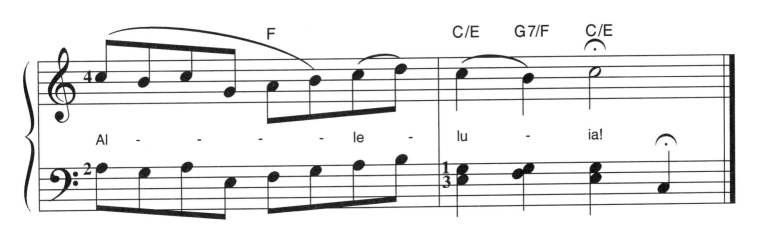

Christ, The Lord, Is Risen Today - 2 - 2

My Faith Looks Up To Thee

RAY PALMER
and LOWELL MASON
Arranged by Richard Bradley